Who eats who in the Desert ?

Andrew Campbell

A⁺
Smart Apple Media

First published in 2005 by Franklin Watts
96 Leonard Street, London EC2A 4XD

Franklin Watts Australia
45–51 Huntley Street, Alexandria NSW 2015

Designer: Cali Roberts, Editor: Constance Novis, Art Director: Peter Scoulding,
Editor-in-Chief: John C. Miles, Picture Research: Diana Morris, Artwork: Ian Thompson

PICTURE CREDITS
John Calcalosi/Still Pictures: 9, 16bl, 21, 24. Brian Cushing/Ecoscene: 14. Michele Depraz/Still Pictures:
12. Nigel J. Dennis/Still Pictures: 27. Xavier Eichaker/Still Pictures: 6, 15, 17. M & P Fogden/FLPA: 7.
Klein/Hubert/Still Pictures: 4b. Wayne Lawler/Ecoscene: 18, 19. Wyman Meinzer/Still Pictures: front
cover, 1, 22. C. Allan Morgan/Still Pictures: 25. Michael Rauch/Still Pictures: 13. Ed Reschke/Still
Pictures: 11. Francois Sauveny/Still Pictures: 26. Roland Seitre/Still Pictures: 8. Raoul Slater/WWI/Still
Pictures: 10. Tom Vezo/Still Pictures: 20. Gordon Wiltsie/Still Pictures: 5t, 16tr. Gunter Ziesler/Still
Pictures: 23.

Published in the United States by Smart Apple Media
2140 Howard Drive West, North Mankato, Minnesota 56003

Library of Congress Cataloging-in-Publication Data

Campbell, Andrew, 1974–
Who eats who in the desert? / by Andrew Campbell.
p. cm. — (Food chains in action)
Originally published: London : Franklin Watts, 2005.
Includes bibliographical references.
ISBN-13 : 978-1-58340-962-6
1. Desert ecology—Juvenile literature. 2. Food chains (Ecology)—Juvenile literature.
I. Title. II. Series.

QH541.5.D4C34 2005
577.54′16—dc22   2005052054

9 8 7 6 5 4 3 2 1

Note to parents and teachers
Every effort has been made to ensure that the Web sites in this book are suitable for children, that they
are of the highest educational value, and that they contain no inappropriate or offensive material.
However, because of the nature of the Internet, it is impossible to guarantee that the contents of these
sites will not be altered. We strongly advise that Internet access be supervised by a responsible adult.

Contents

Life in the desert

Deserts are extreme places. They can be very hot during the day and very cold at night. They can also be very dry. In South America's Atacama Desert, for example, it rained only 4 times in 100 years.

Extreme landscapes

The landscape of the desert is affected by the great range of temperatures. Very few plants can survive in such a wide range of hot, dry, and cold conditions. Some landscapes are made up of endless sand dunes or large rocks. Only a few types of grasses, trees, or bushes can be found growing there.

Survival

Because deserts are such extreme places, the plants, animals, and people that live there have to depend on each other in order to survive.

In the Sahàra Desert in Africa—the largest desert on Earth—goats survive by eating whatever grasses are available. In turn, people living there, known as Bedouins, drink goats' milk.

Yummy!

The camel spider lives in deserts around the world and can grow up to six inches (15 cm) long. It likes to catch and eat lizards and small birds.

4

We're in the chain!

Nomads are people who have survived in deserts for thousands of years. In Africa, nomads such as the Bedouin people keep herds of goats and camels, which they rely on for milk and meat.

Habitats and food chains

All organisms (living things) require a place to live where they can find everything necessary for survival. This place is known as a habitat. Within every habitat exist food chains. These are simple lists showing the links between who eats what or whom. By looking at a food chain, you can see how each part of the chain helps to keep the next part alive.

The moloch lizard, or thorny devil, of Australia has adapted to survive in one of the world's most extreme environments.

Who Eats Who?

grass

goat

Bedouin drinks goat's milk

From chains to webs

A food chain shows how one animal eats one type of plant or one other animal. But in the desert, where there might be little food, most animals have to eat whatever they can find. This means they depend on lots of different plants and animals— a relationship called a food web.

Yummy!

The Australian skink, a type of lizard that lives in the desert, has a very mixed diet. It eats spiders, cockroaches, centipedes, beetles, termites, ants, grasshoppers, crickets, and silverfish.

A food web in action

A food web shows how different food chains are connected. For example, the houbara bustard, which lives in the deserts of Central Asia, is part of many different food chains. This is because it eats plant seeds and shoots, as well as locusts, beetles, and lizards.

All of these animals can be linked together in a food web. If the bustard could not find seeds, it might eat more beetles. This would leave fewer beetles for animals in other food chains to eat.

Houbara bustard.

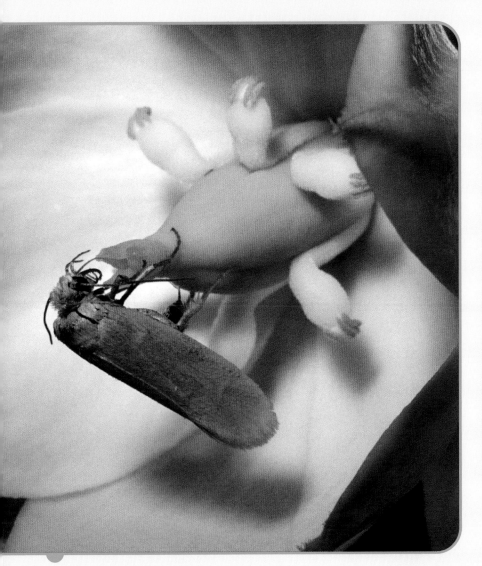

A desert yucca moth perches on a yucca flower.

Wet and dry webs

Weather has a great effect on food chains and food webs in the desert. In very dry weather, a lizard might eat seeds or small insects. When rain does finally arrive, plants burst into life and grow. Animals breed or travel into the desert to look for food, which gives the lizard more choice in what it eats.

Fussy eaters

Most desert animals eat whatever they can. However, some creatures are fussy. In the deserts of the United States, for example, the yucca moth only eats the yucca plant; the female moth lays its eggs on the plant. But the yucca plant depends on the yucca moth, too. Every time the female visits a yucca plant, it spreads pollen from one yucca to another. This allows the yucca plant to reproduce.

Desert plants

Plants are the first link in any food chain, since they make their energy directly from sunlight through photosynthesis. This energy is available to other living things higher up the food chain.

Strong sunlight

Unlike plants elsewhere, desert plants face a unique problem—too much sunlight! In strong sunlight, people often wear light-colored clothes that reflect the sun and keep them cool. Many desert plants use the same idea. They have pale green or gray stems and branches to reflect the sunlight.

Ephemeral plants

Some plants, called ephemerals, spend most of the time lying in the ground as seeds. When it rains, the seeds burst into life, producing leaves in as little as two hours.

The plants flower briefly, then die, leaving more seeds to lie in wait for the next rains. Ephemerals can produce 600 million seeds per acre (0.4 ha) of desert!

Desert in bloom after rain, South Africa.

We're in the chain!

The San people, who live in Africa's Kalahari Desert, eat wild watermelons and cucumbers. The plants are an important source of water and vitamin C.

Yummy!

When ephemeral plants blossom after rain, honey ants feed some of their workers plant nectar until their bodies swell up. The other ants use the swollen workers as food containers and suck the nectar from them. Honey ants are eaten by lizards, who are in turn eaten by birds of prey such as hawks.

This huge saguaro cactus grows in the southwestern U.S.

Perennial plants

Plants that stay alive all the time are called perennials. Desert perennials include tough grasses. In very dry times, the grasses look dead, but their long roots are still alive under the ground. Other perennials are cactus plants, which grow in North and South America. After it has rained, cacti can store huge amounts of water in their stems, which swell like balloons.

Who Eats Who?

prickly pear (fruit)

worker honey ant

other honey ants eat nectar stored in worker

horned lizard

hawk

Eating it up

The first animal in a food chain is always a herbivore—a plant-eater. Herbivores in the desert range in size from tiny insects to big mammals, such as antelopes and kangaroos.

Small animal food chains

A female kangaroo and her baby, called a joey.

In the driest deserts, there are few plants, so herbivores have to eat seeds or bits of plants blown into the desert on the wind. Deserts like this only have enough food for tiny plant-eaters, such as insects.

The next animals in food chains are carnivores—meat-eaters. In very dry deserts, the carnivores are small spiders or lizards, or small rodents. Other carnivores, such as snakes and birds, eat these animals.

Bigger animal food chains

Deserts with more plant life support larger herbivores. In Africa, deer-like mammals called gazelles get all the food and water they need from desert plants—some species go their entire lives without drinking water.

Bigger herbivores attract bigger carnivores. Desert animals that hunt gazelles are jackals, hyenas, and wild cats called caracals, which have short tails and pointed, tufted ears.

This wily coyote of the southwestern U.S. is an omnivore—it has a varied diet.

Yummy!

Australian kangaroos eat leaves, grass, and roots. They are specially adapted for extreme survival and can go months without drinking.

Yummy!

The leaves of a desert plant called the creosote bush contain a poisonous oil to prevent animals from nibbling it. But the creosote bush grasshopper doesn't mind the poison—the leaves are its favorite food.

Omnivores

Many desert animals are not purely herbivores or carnivores, but omnivores—they eat everything! In the Mojave Desert in the U.S., wild dogs called coyotes eat rabbits, rodents, antelopes, and goats. But they are also happy to eat plants, especially the seed pods of the mesquite tree.

Breaking it down

When a living thing produces waste or dies, animals called decomposers break it down. The broken-down matter then provides nutrients that help plants grow.

About decomposers

When a plant or animal dies, many animals will not eat it. But microorganisms such as bacteria and fungi, known as decomposers, attack the dead matter. They eat it and begin to break it down.

In the desert, decomposers include beetles, earthworms, and millipedes. These animals feed on dead and decaying bits of plants or animals that they find on or underneath the surface of the desert.

We're in the chain!

In Africa, people fry or roast winged termites, or grind them into a flour. Queen termites, in particular, are considered a delicacy.

A termite nest.

Termites

Some of the most important desert decomposers are small insects called termites. They have soft, pale bodies and look like ants, but they are more closely related to cockroaches.

Most termites live underground in groups, called colonies, and eat a variety of dead material. Australian scientists have found that desert termites there eat dead grasses, leaves, roots, wood, and sheep and kangaroo dung.

Smaller decomposers

After beetles, earthworms, and termites have eaten the dead plant or animal material, most of it passes out of their bodies into the soil. But now it is in much smaller pieces, ready for even tinier animals to eat.

These microorganisms include nematode worms and protozoans, which can be less than 0.0004 inches (0.01 mm) long. These decomposers break down waste, releasing minerals that help new plants grow.

Who Eats Who?

camel dung

scarab beetle

termite (eats beetle's waste)

nematode worm (eats termite's waste)

new plant (helped to grow by minerals released by broken-down dung)

Dung beetle.

Yummy!

African dung beetles gather up the dung of animals such as camels and goats and roll it into balls. The beetle buries the ball underground and later feeds on it.

The desert at night

When the temperature drops at night, the desert comes alive with activity. Many animals emerge to look for seeds, nibble on plants, or hunt other creatures.

The fennec fox

In the Sahara Desert lives a small mammal weighing less than a pet cat. It is a type of fox called a fennec (right), and it comes out at night to catch lizards, insects, and rodents such as gerbils.

The fennec is well-adapted to nighttime hunting. It has a good sense of smell and huge ears that pick up the tiniest noises of its prey. During the day, the fennec's big ears also help its body heat escape.

Keeping cool

Mammals are warm-blooded. This means their bodies always stay at the same temperature. Most desert mammals, including rodents, rabbits, foxes, and cats, are nocturnal—they are active at night.

The reason for this is that warm-blooded mammals feel comfortable in the chilly desert night, but they can overheat during the day. To avoid this, many animals spend the daytime sleeping in cool underground burrows or beneath rocks.

An angry scorpion holds its tail up, ready to strike.

Yummy!

The ningaui is a tiny rodent that lives in Australia's deserts. It weighs only 0.14 ounces (4 g), but it is an aggressive night hunter. The ningaui's two favorite meals—desert centipedes and cockroaches—are bigger than it is!

Insects, spiders, and scorpions

Many smaller desert creatures, such as flies, ants, grasshoppers, and spiders, are also active at night. Scorpions can survive fiercer heat than insects, but they too are nocturnal.

Some scorpions are four and three-quarters inches (12 cm) long. They are bold hunters and catch spiders, insects, and other scorpions with their powerful pincers before killing them with the poison stinger in their tail. The poison from some scorpions is so strong that it can kill a person in a few hours.

Daytime desert

Daytime desert food chains are made up of animals whose bodies can withstand the scorching, dry heat.

Reptiles rule

The kings of the daytime desert—lizards, snakes, and tortoises—are reptiles. Unlike mammals, reptiles are cold-blooded. Their body temperature changes according to their surroundings.

At night, when desert temperatures drop, reptiles lose their body heat and have little energy for hunting. In the daytime, however, the heat of the sun warms them up, giving them the energy to look for food.

A blazing daytime desert scene.

Western diamondback rattlesnake.

Lizards and tortoises

The largest lizard of all is the desert monitor lizard. It lives in Africa and Asia and grows to five and a quarter feet (1.6 m). A much smaller lizard is the spiny-tailed lizard of northern Africa, which reaches about one foot (30 cm).

Most lizards and snakes are carnivores, but tortoises are herbivores. The desert tortoise of the U.S. can store nearly two pints (1 L) of water in its body just from the plants it eats, and it survives on this liquid during dry times.

Spiny-tailed lizard.

Yummy!

The Egyptian spiny-tailed lizard likes to eat both plant matter and insects, such as crickets. Its armored tail keeps predators away.

We're in the chain!

Although their traditional ways are becoming much less common, some San people in the Kalahari Desert still hunt animals such as antelope using bows and poisoned arrows, as well as with animal traps.

Daytime mammals

Not all desert mammals come out at night. Many large mammals cope with the heat better than smaller ones, and some, such as antelopes, camels, and kangaroos, are too big to find shelter from the sun.

Antelopes can withstand increases in their body temperature even though they are warm-blooded. And a camel's thick fur coat actually acts as a shield against the sun.

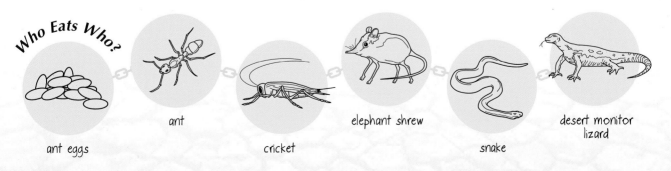

Who Eats Who?

ant eggs — ant — cricket — elephant shrew — snake — desert monitor lizard

Life in the sand

Sandy desert regions provide animals with a cool place to burrow and hide from the sun. But the sand is not always safe—expert hunters are never far away.

Small sand dwellers

Smaller creatures that live in the sand include camel crickets, scorpions, beetles, cockroaches, and spiders. These animals don't burrow just for the cooler temperatures there, but because they know they may be able to find water or the remains of plant or animal matter beneath the surface. One fearsome insect that hunts in the sand is the larva of the ant lion. It digs a pit in the sand, covers itself with more sand, waits for another insect to slide down into the hole, and then eats it.

Ant lion larva.

Young bearded dragon lizard.

Bigger sand dwellers

A bigger animal that eats insects that burrow in the sand is the legless skink lizard of Africa's Namib Desert. The skink moves through the sand by wriggling.

In Australia, the bearded dragon lizard grows to about 20 inches (50 cm). It is an expert hunter, eating all kinds of smaller sand-dwelling creatures.

Snakes

Many snakes are also very good at hunting in the sand, but they move across the surface rather than burrowing into it. Sidewinding snakes move by slithering sideways.

The sidewinding adder of the Namib Desert plays a hunting trick. The only part of the snake's body visible above the sand is its tail. It moves its tail to imitate an insect, which attracts unwary lizards.

Life on a plant

Some desert plants are a home to many different animals and contain entire food chains. This is especially true of the saguaro cactus and the desert ironwood tree, both found in the deserts of the southwestern U.S.

Saguaro cactus

The saguaro cactus is the tallest of all cactus plants, growing up to 50 feet (15 m) in height. Despite its poisonous, prickly spines, many animals live on or in the saguaro.

Desert woodpeckers make holes in the top of the plant, in which they build nests. Cactus pygmy owls, which are small enough to fit into a person's hand, often move into these nests when the woodpeckers have left. The owls hunt other birds, lizards, rodents, and insects that live on or near the cactus.

This desert woodpecker nests in a saguaro cactus.

We're in the chain!

Native Americans have traditionally ground up the seeds of the desert ironwood tree and eaten them. They have also used the tree's flowers and roots for medicines.

A cactus pygmy owl and its chicks in their nest in the middle of a saguaro cactus.

Ironwood chain

Desert ironwood trees support around 500 plant and animal species in their native region of the Sonoran Desert in the U.S. The ironwood's leaves give shade to many creatures. Most years, the tree produces hard seed pods, which rodents such as the kangaroo rat like to break open and eat. Kangaroo rats, in turn, are eaten by long-nosed snakes, and snakes by kit foxes and other larger mammals.

Helping other plants

The desert ironwood also offers shade to smaller plants, such as cacti and wildflowers, and protects them from cold temperatures at night. The plants that grow underneath ironwoods attract more animals to feed there, including jackrabbits, desert bighorn sheep, and deer.

Who Eats Who?

ironwood seeds

kangaroo rat

long-nosed snake

kit fox

From the ground to the air

Birds and flying insects have a big advantage over other desert animals. They can travel farther to hunt whatever food is available.

Desert birds

In Australia, desert birds include brightly colored parrots, as well as the Australian bustard, which grabs lizards and rodents with its sharp beak and swallows them whole. The roadrunner of the southwestern U.S. prefers to walk rather than fly. It eats insects, scorpions, lizards, and even rattlesnakes.

In Africa and the U.S., two large birds that often fly over deserts are the golden eagle and the vulture. All eagles kill their own prey, but vultures are scavengers, so they look for animals that are dead already.

Cooling down

Because flying creates a lot of heat, birds are used to high body temperatures. Their feathers provide protection from the sun's rays, and many birds also cool down by fluttering the skin on their throats—just like we use a fan.

Reptile snack: a roadrunner devours a lizard.

Locusts gather together in huge swarms.

Locusts

Insects such as flies, wasps, crickets, and butterflies also fly over the desert. But the best-known flying desert insects are locusts. Locusts fly together in huge groups, or swarms, of up to 40 billion.

As they fly, locusts are pulled by low air pressure to places where it has rained and plants are growing. Swarms can eat up all the plants in an area of desert. This can seriously affect food chains and webs for other animals and ruin farm crops.

A watery food chain

Rain showers in the desert cause new life to burst out and trigger short-lived food chains. One of these chains involves the amazing spadefoot toad of the Arizona Desert in the U.S.

Spadefoot toads

Most toads like damp places, so they are not natural desert dwellers. The spadefoot toad is different. It hides in a burrow that it digs under the ground with its hind feet.

After a rare desert rain shower, the spadefoot emerges into daylight. Male and female toads mate, and the female lays her eggs in a shallow pool that the rain has made.

Race for survival

As soon as the eggs hatch into tadpoles, the race begins for them to grow into adults before their watery home in the pool dries up. This is because an adult toad can live out of water, but a tadpole cannot.

The pools are full of algae, water fleas, and tiny shrimp that come to life when it rains. All are food for the tadpoles.

Spadefoot toad.

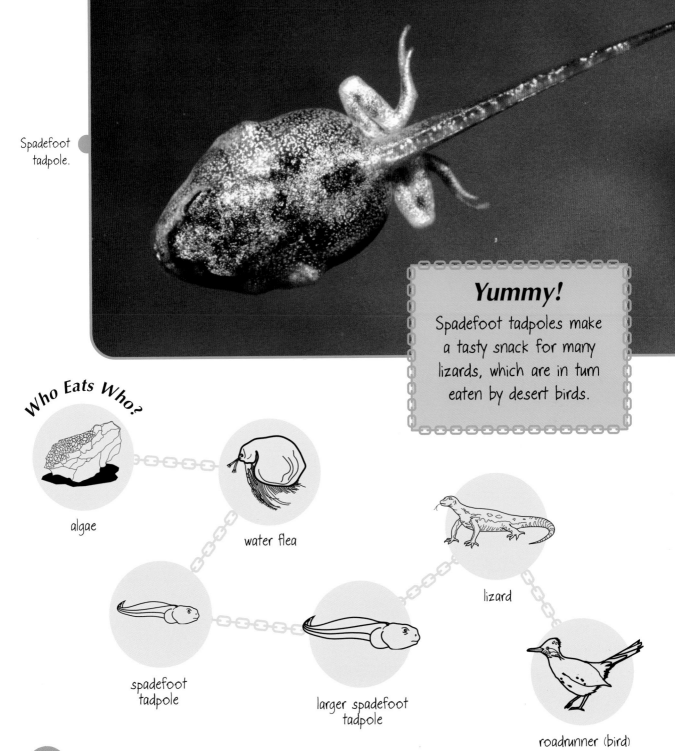

Spadefoot tadpole.

Yummy!

Spadefoot tadpoles make a tasty snack for many lizards, which are in turn eaten by desert birds.

Who Eats Who?

algae → water flea

spadefoot tadpole → larger spadefoot tadpole → lizard → roadrunner (bird)

Tadpoles eating tadpoles

The pools can also contain larger shrimps called fairy shrimp. If there are fairy shrimp around, some tadpoles develop bigger heads and mouths to eat them. And the bigger tadpoles don't stop there—they start to eat the smaller tadpoles, too. This means the bigger tadpoles can become toads even more quickly, which might be vital if the pool is fast drying out.

On the edge of the desert

Many deserts are surrounded by grasslands or mountains. While these areas are still hot and dry, they receive more rain than deserts themselves and attract more plants and animals.

Savanna

On the edge of many deserts lies a region of grasses and scattered trees known as savanna. In Africa, herds of antelopes and gazelles often roam this region. But they must stay on the alert for the animals that hunt them, such as lions, leopards, cheetahs, and caracals.

Lion.

We're in the chain!

As people build more homes and cities on the edge of deserts, animals must adapt to their new surroundings. In cities on the edge of deserts in the southwestern U.S., for example, coyotes often eat scraps of food from garbage cans.

Staying together

Many antelopes and gazelles stay in large herds for safety. Most young antelopes are born around the same time for the same reason. If they were born throughout the year, the big cats would have a constant supply of vulnerable prey.

Many antelopes wander deep into the desert after it rains, when more plants grow. At such times, lions and other predators follow them, in search of a meal.

Rare rhinoceroses

The region around the Namib Desert in southwest Africa has both flat savanna and high mountains. It is home to many endangered animals, such as the mountain zebra and the black rhinoceros. Like the zebra, the rhinoceros is a herbivore, feeding on grasses and woody plants. Rhinoceroses have few predators—aside from people, who have killed them in large numbers for their horns.

Who Eats Who?

leaf

springbok (gazelle)

leopard

A springbok in a South African desert setting.

Yummy!

Birds such as oxpeckers spend a lot of their time on rhinoceroses' backs, eating the small insects that make their home there.

Food web

Here is a typical desert food web, along with some fascinating desert facts.

Deserts and semi-deserts make up nearly one-third of Earth's land area.

Some desert animals, including fennec foxes and certain scorpions, obtain all the water they need from the animals they kill.

tortoise

decomposers (bacteria, fungi, insects, earthworms, protozoans, and nematode worms)

desert plants (perennials and ephemerals)

insects

To find water deep underground, the roots of the camelthorn acacia tree, which grows in African deserts, can reach down 100 feet (30.5 m).

The hottest air temperature ever recorded was in the Sahara Desert in Libya in 1922. It was 136 °F (57.8 °C).

herbivores, mammals, and birds

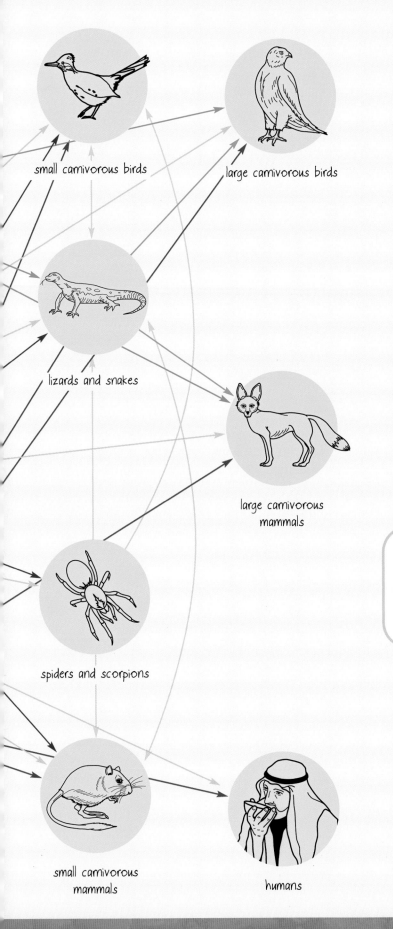

small carnivorous birds

large carnivorous birds

lizards and snakes

large carnivorous
mammals

spiders and scorpions

small carnivorous
mammals

humans

The date palm tree
is a very important plant
for people living in the
deserts of North Africa
and the Middle East. They
eat its fruit (dates) and
use its wood for houses
and its leaves for fences,
baskets, and sandals.

Fairy shrimp eggs can
blow with the desert dust for
50 years before rains cause the
shrimp to hatch and grow.

Some bristlecone pine
trees, which grow in the deserts
of North America, have been
alive for about 5,000 years.

Scientists think
there are around 1,200
different types of plants
in the Sahara Desert
and about 40 different
kinds of rodents!

Glossary

algae

very simple kinds of plants that do not have stems, roots, or leaves.

bacteria

tiny, one-celled microorganisms that live in soil, as well as in water, plants, and animals' bodies.

carnivore

a meat-eating animal.

cold-blooded

an animal whose body temperature is linked to the outside temperature. At night, when it is cold, cold-blooded animals are also cold. When the sun rises, they warm up. Insects, spiders, fish, amphibians, and reptiles are all cold-blooded.

decomposer

a living thing that feeds on and breaks down dead plants and animals, as well as animal waste.

desert

a region with few plants and trees, where it rarely rains. One definition of a desert is a place that receives less than 10 inches (25 cm) of rain each year.

ephemerals

plants that live for a very short time. In the desert, ephemeral plants remain lifeless as seeds until it rains. They quickly sprout roots, flower, and produce seeds.

fungus

a type of organism (the plural is "fungi") that lives on dead or rotting things. Mold and mushrooms are both types of fungi.

herbivore

an animal that eats plants.

larva

the young form (the plural is "larvae") of some insects that looks quite different from the adults.

microorganism

a living thing that is so small it can only be seen under a microscope.

nectar

a sweet, energy-rich liquid produced by flowers to attract pollinating animals such as bees.

nocturnal

describes an animal that comes out at night to eat and perform other activities, such as hunting.

nomad

a member of a group of people who move their home from place to place in search of good land on which their herds of animals can feed.

omnivore

an animal that eats plants and other animals.

perennials

plants that survive year-round, and sometimes for many, many years. Some desert perennial plants are around 5,000 years old.

photosynthesis

the process by which plants capture the energy of sunlight to make sugar.

pollen

tiny, dust-like specks in a flower that make plant seeds grow.

predator

an animal that kills and eats other animals.

savanna

an area of grassland that contains scattered trees or bushes. Some savanna regions are on the edge of deserts.

scavenger

an animal that eats dead or dying things, including leftovers from another animal's meal. Decomposers are scavengers, but the best-known are vultures.

warm-blooded

animals that maintain the same body temperature when it is hot or cold outside.

Desert Web Sites

http://www.desertmuseum.org/kids
Information about deserts from the Desert Museum in Arizona.

www.ucmp.berkeley.edu/glossary/gloss5/biome/deserts.html
All about deserts, from the University of California at Berkeley.

http://digital-desert.com/wildlife
Lots of good information about U.S. desert wildlife.

Index